TO MY CAPRICIOUS LOVE

To My Capricious Love

Love Poems of a Romantic Journey of Unrequited Love

BY MONICA M. CULQUI

Illustrations by the author from the photography of Barbara Powers

Published by

CloseKnit Books

232 W. Washington Street

Madison, Georgia 30650

To My Capricious Love

ISBN 978-0-615-34575-8

First Edition

Book design by burt&burt

burtandburt.com

Printed in Canada

Author's Note

Often we are unable to recognize the beauty of suffering, because only when one suffers can the joy of happiness be measured to its optimum. We, sometimes, do not appreciate that at one point in our lives, all of us are bestowed with love and affection—and with the pleasures of the flesh. It is important to recognize and accept that these are gifts and as they are given they can also be taken away, causing suffering which at the moment it happens, might seem as an eternity. However, the human heart is very resilient and the human spirit is far stronger than we give it credit for.

It was not until I was able to recognize that each day the sun rises and the sun sets; and the experience of loving, suffering, longing, and more loving is the life that happens in between. Only then was I able to recount the emotions felt by writing these poems in that spirit of strength and resilience knowing that unrequited love does not kill.

Dear reader, enjoy the experiences of a life well lived thus far, and in the words of my favorite Hispanic author, El maestro Don Gabriel Garcia Marquez, *"La Vida hay que Vivirla para Contarla."*

To life!
Mónica M. Culqui Flores

Acknowledgments

Thank you to Barbara P., my best friend,
my creative cohort,
my loving sounding board,
my guiding light in the darkest moments of this past year;
to Adria Jehan, the love of my life,
who has brought me the greatest passion from the day she was born;
to my family for always letting me dream,
and to the people who have rejoiced and suffered
from an unrequited love.

To the muse,

who oftentimes
left me in the middle of the night
to peruse through the corners of my soul,
for these pages to become;
thank you for stealing the kiss
and letting me see myself
in the splendor of your blue eyes.

NOTHING'S BEEN THE SAME *15*

NO ONE KNOWS *17*   YOUR ARRIVAL *19*   YOUR TOUCH *21*

EL SECRETO *23*   THE LEAF *25*   I WANT *27*

SLICES OF HEAVEN *29*   THE BEAUTY IN YOUR EYES *30*

OUR NIGHTS *33*   CONTENTS OF MY HEART *35*   YOU *37*

UNREACHABLE YOU *38*   MI DOLOR, MI PAZ *41*

FOR YOU, THE THRILL IS GONE *42*

TE QUIERO! *45*   FULL MOON *47*   A THOUSAND DEATHS *49*

YOUR ARROGANCE *51*   NOCHE SIN FÍN *53*   THROUGH MY FINGERS *55*

A FORGOTTEN DREAM *56*   WITHOUT A THOUGHT *59*

HASTA LA MUERTE *60*   REMEMBRANCE *63*   PIERCING DAGGER *65*

GIVING LOVE A CHANCE *67*

LAST POEM *69*   ADIEU *70*

Spanish Translations *73*

To My
Capricious
Love

Nothing's Been the Same

Serendipity brought you to my arms
I stole a kiss, I lost my soul,
your kiss, my fountain of youth,
your eyes, the clearest of skies,
your happiness, my greatest joy,
caught up in the enchantment of being with you,
nothing's been the same.

No One Knows

Under a beckoning moon
a kiss was given,
full of lust, full of wanting and beseeching.

Your eyes captivated my soul,
your smile brought me joy,
your kiss, pure rapture.

What damaging nature
this wondrous and lustful moment possessed,
no one knows.

Your Arrival

In the alcove of my soul, very quietly,
    I await for your arrival.

Once in my arms,
    our hearts will resonate as movements of the sweetest symphony,
in its melodic rhythm your body will rejoice of mine,
    bringing to a crescendo our moment in time.

            Prisoner of your love, I will gladly become
                delving into the sweet euphoria of your touch,
            etched forevermore in the penumbra of my heart,
                where quietly I will always wait for your return.

Your Touch

The smell of us enshrouds my bed,

the taste of your love lingers on my lips,

your cries of ecstacy echo in my ear,

your smile a pleasurable sight to my heart's content,

your touch awakens my soul.

Only with you, I feel alive.

El Secreto

El secreto de tenerte unos ratos en mi alcoba,
    será la muerte
que vendrá en la alborada,
    pasando en mi pobre corazón
la mas fuerte puñalada,
    cuando el último beso me lo des
bajo la almoada,
    que tantos ratos en secreto
me vio amarte apasionadamente.

The Leaf

Before the flames
    engulf the dry and dead leaf,
the heat brings it back to its original shape,
    restoring it anew;

Before engulfing it to death with its fiery force,
    it is alive only to be consumed,
bringing it to ashes and nothingness;

Everytime we kiss, I become the leaf.

I Want

In your eyes,
>   I want to see me smile.

From your mouth,
>   I want the kiss that brings new life.

In your embrace,
>   I want the refuge bringing me solace.

From your soul,
>   I want your tenderness as sweet as I know it can be.

In your heart,
>   I want to remain till the end of days.

Slices of Heaven

Slices of heaven,
 I call the moments when I am with you,
embracing, touching,
 feeling the tumultous wave of fire
passing through my veins,
 comforting my soul, blowing my mind,
changing me entirely into something so good,
 I ache when you leave.

The Beauty in Your Eyes

To see the beauty I found in your eyes,
to feel the warmth of your embrace,
to rejoice of your pleasure when you came in my arms,
was to savor life at its sweetest.

I do not know when I lost my way,
    but in your arms I found my soul,
in your embrace my wanting you
    became more and more as your scent remained
in the deep corners of my being.

        I know I should not miss you,
           nor have the many thoughts of you,
        but I do,
           and only hope that somehow
        I am also in your thoughts,
           caressing you, touching you,
        finding the beauty I found in your eyes.

Our Nights

You came in the darkness of my lonely nights
    to illuminate my days,
to give me peace in a world of uncertainty and dismay,
    to let me see the beauty of your soul in a world of chaos and disdain.

I quietly shall love you in all days of my life,
        waiting for you to come
    to encompass my life with yours
        in the stillness of our nights.

Contents of *My Heart*

Let me love you from afar
without disclosing the contents of my heart.

Let me be there for you.

Let me be your shelter in the storm,
your comfort in moments of despair,
your strength when weakness abounds.

Let me love you from afar,
knowing in my arms you'll always find
that the contents of my heart only belong to you.

You

Your hair
    sacred relics in my heart,

your eyes
    my heaven on earth,

your kiss
    engulfing fire that brings me life,

you
    the goodness of my soul,
despite your inability to see.

Till the end of days
    I want to keep you close
despite your stubborn need
    to be so far away from me.

Unreachable You

I'd like to say that perhaps one day,
   we will rest in each other's arms,
going to places no one knows about,
   going to heaven only to be brought down by a quotidian life.

I'd love to say that perhaps one day,
   we will have our moments in time,
going to places we've already been,
   going to heaven only to stay in the pure bliss of our kiss.

I'd rather not say that one day,
    I know you will bid adieu to our moments and my love.

        Only then will I go to places where no one would know of me
            or of the pleasure that was to see me in your eyes,
        how much I enjoyed the sweetness of your lips,
            and the warmth of your body lying next to mine.

            Then heaven will become a place as unreachable as you are to me.

Mi Dolor, Mi Paz

Ave de amor y paz eres,
    por el viento te vas sin dejar huellas,
ya que tu corazón nunca amó por no dejar de ser como eres,
    ave de fuego fugaz te vas solo sin penas,
ya que tu alma cansada no quiere dejar huellas.

    Ave de amor y dolor eres,
        te vas con el viento hacia el caer del día sin dejar huellas
    de tu alma perdida,
        de tu alma dolida por no dejar de ser como eres,
    mi ave de amor eres y es por eso que en tus ojos
        encontré mi dolor, encontré mi paz.

For You, the Thrill Is Gone

For you, the thrill is gone,
    but your sweet scent remains,
making me long for you,
    making me want you the more.

For you, the thrill is gone,
    so is my heart, it's gone, lost,
 only succumbing to the beat of yours.

For you, the thrill is gone,
     so it seems, but truth be told,
deep down running through my veins,
    you are my thrill, bringing the desire,
bringing that tumultous passionate fire
    that keeps me longing,
waiting,
    until you come to me
to quench that thirst
    that will never, ever be gone.

Te Quiero!

Nuestro amor lo reservas para la noche
    porque no tienes la bravia para quererme en el día,
te arrenpentirás un día cuando al salir el sol
    te des cuenta que ya no estoy ahi,
que fisícamente
    el calor de mi cuerpo estará lejos de ti,
yo no estaré mas ahi,
    pero mi alma, mis pensamientos,
mi dulce quererte siempre, siempre estarán contigo,
    Te quiero!

Full Moon

It's a full moon and it makes me want to shout
how much I love to have you under my sheets
suckling my breasts, tasting the passion long ago suppressed.

Alas! Adding to the sadness of it all,
because I am going to remember all our moments,
long for your caress and your kisses,
adore you till the end of days.

A thousand deaths I will die
 longing for your love.
A thousand deaths I will die
 wanting you to be the one
I lay down at the end of the day.

A thousand deaths I will die
 to caress your sweet face,
kiss your lips,
 and know that in my embrace
you find the peace,
 you find the love,
that exalts us to a place
 where only you and I exist.

Your Arrogance

I can no longer bear crying every night
   at the thought of not having you;
I can no longer ignore your unwillingness to see the love
   bestowed upon your lightning blue eyes.

Those eyes that stole a kiss,
   that stole my soul,
only to be dismissed with your arrogance,
   brought by the void in your heart,
preventing you to see all the wonders,
   the promise of my love for you can bring.

Noche Sin Fín

Un día amé con mi alma entera,
y me quedé sola en la espera.

Tu amor nunca me llegó
y entre sollozos,
en la más triste penumbra,
el viento mi alma se llevó
hacía la marea más negra y turbulante
de una noche sin fín.

Through My Fingers

With each passing day that I do not hold you near me,
my heart aches, and the feelings I hold so dear
seem to become like water slipping through my fingers.

The tears on my cheeks have the same salty taste,
a reminder of your love
I no longer have near me.

Forgotten Dream

In a long forgotten dream,
    you and I perhaps could have been,
because you showed me how deliciously
    your touch can awaken my senses,
and how easily I can be lost in your caress.

Only to realize, it was only a dream,
    because you also showed me how costly
being by your side could be,
    how painfully your arrogance and indifference
could easily destroy my heart.

In the reality of my sadness,
    I can see the many wondrous things you showed me,
captivating my soul till eternity,
    yet deliberately forgetting to show me
how to live without you.

Without a Thought

Your embrace dispelled a certain loneliness,
    your kiss saw the last of my innocence,
you awoke the fiery passion long ago contained
    in your touch, losing all my senses,
and without a thought, the goodness of my heart,
    I let go.

Hasta la Muerte

Mi pasión ardiente
   es quererte hasta la muerte,
el no verte
   me quita el sueño,
el no tenerte
   me rompe el alma.

Asi, dolida y desolada
    paso los días
con mi alma camino a la locura
    por no dejar de sentir
ese amor puro y tierno
    que tu desdén abandonó en la alborada.

Sigo amándote, sigo anhelándote
    y con este loco amor mio
te adoraré apasionadamente,
    ardientemente
hasta la muerte.

Remembrance

Lost in a careless kiss,
    saved by the indifference of an arrogant love.

Lost in his touch,
    saved by the pain of his disdain.

Lost in his lustful embrace,
    saved by Divine grace
that places a smile on my face
    at the remembrance of what could have been.

Piercing Dagger

Mercilessly you thrust a piercing dagger
    through my vulnerable heart,
with the promise of giving me
    a new morn wrapped in your embrace,
only to be taken away in exchange
    for a fleeting moment of the flesh.

I knew then, as reality faces me now,
    that in your arms I will never awaken
to celebrate the day.

    Instead, the burning pain of your disdain will stay in my heart
as the piercing dagger you've planted today.

Giving Love a Chance

The day will come when I will rejoice of a new lover's embrace,
    full of love, full of passion,
having eyes only for our hearth.

The day will come when I will rejoice of a friend's embrace,
    full of trust, full of sincere love and affection,
having only loving eyes
    remembering our previous night of passion.

The day will come when I will rejoice of someone else's love,
    ready to wake up in a morning anew
to give friendship, to give life, to give love a chance.

Last Poem

The tears flow while I sit among the shelves full of books.
　　Tennyson's poetry in bright purple binding looks down on me.
OVID in its yellow splendor spine smiles.

And essays,
　　essays are the rhythm in my eyes as I sit sadly thinking
how your love took away the laughter,
　　took away the joy,
feeling void of any romantic emotion, I wipe the tears away,
　　pondering words to write the last poem to your engulfing eyes,
careless kiss,
　　that only left sweet bitter emotions behind.

Adieu

In the dark stillness of my sleepless nights,
   you came with a sweet caress and an engulfing kiss,
filling my heart with joy,
   bringing me hope and a new morn.

My sleepless nights will never be the same,
    the darkness dissipated by the moonlight will forever remind me
how I fell under the spell of your kiss,
    bringing joy and music to my tired soul.

        With this new-found hope,
            I will raise my eyes to the blue sky of each new morn
        and think how in those sweet blue eyes of yours
          I saw myself come alive.

But all good things come to an end,
    and I must bid adieu
to your kisses and caress,
    for now I know, they were never mine to keep.

Translations

On the following pages are the translations to the five Spanish poems.

El Secreto (The Secret)

The secret of having those fleeting moments with you in my chambers
    will be my death that will come at dawn,
piercing through my poor heart
    the lethal blow,
when you kiss me for the last time
    on the soft pillow that many nights saw me loving you passionately,
in the numerous secret fleeting moments of ours.

Mi Dolor, Mi Paz (My Suffering, My Peace)

You are my bird of love and peace
    that flees behind the wind without any trace,
your heart never loved
    because you did not want to change who you are.

You are my bird of a fleeting fire that leaves alone
    without any sorrows
because your tired soul does not want to leave any traces.

You are my bird of love and pain
    that flees behind the wind at dusk
without any trace of your lost soul
    or your pain
because you do not want to change who you are.

You are my bird of love and in your eyes
    I found my suffering, I found my peace.

Te Quiero! (I Love You!)

You reserve our love for the night
    because you do not have the courage to love me in the day,
you will regret it one day
    at the break of dawn
when you realize that I am no longer there,
    that physically
the warmth of my body will be
    far away from you.

I will no longer be there
    but my soul, my thoughts,
my sweet and fervently way of loving you
    will always be yours,
I Love You!

Noche Sin Fín (Endless Night)

I once loved you whole heartedly and
    I remained alone waiting for your response.
Your love never arrived and
    in between sullen and sad whimpers
in the darkest of nights
    the wind took my soul
toward the darkest
    and most turbulent high sea of an endless night.

Hasta la Muerte (Till the Day I Die)

My ardent passion is to love you till the day I die,
 not to see you becomes my sleepless nights,
not to have you becomes my tortured soul.

Feeling hurt and desolate
 I go through my days
on the verge of losing my soul to madness
 because I choose not to let go of the pure and tender love
that you arrogantly abandoned at dawn.

I will continue to love and yearn for you
 and with this crazy love of mine
I will adore you passionately,
 ardently,
till the day I die.